DECORATING BASICS

FOR MEN ONLY

Gloria Hander Lyons

Blue Sage Press

DECORATING BASICS
FOR MEN ONLY

Inquires should be addressed to:
Blue Sage Press
48 Borondo Pines
La Marque, TX 77568
www.BlueSagePress.com

ISBN: 978-0-9790618-9-9

Library of Congress Control Number: 2007908760

First Edition: December, 2007

Printed in the United States of America

Table of Contents

Introduction

DECORATING BASICS FOR MEN ONLY!

Whether single, divorced or widowed, there are millions of men who live alone, and, like everyone else, you want your home to be comfortable, functional and attractive.

Our homes should be a place where we can relax and surround ourselves with the things we enjoy. This takes a bit of planning and, well, decorating. The term "decorating" is downright scary to most men because it sounds complicated and restrictive—no fun intended nor implied.

But take heart, guys, this book is a no-frills, down-to-basics manual that offers helpful tips for clearing out the clutter, practical advice for making your rooms more functional, and a step-by-step guide for creating an attractive, comfortable living space that you'll be proud to show off to friends and family.

An added bonus—you'll score extra points with the ladies. Women like men who have attractive, organized homes.

In just a few easy steps, your home can go from "Blah" to "Wow!"

For the most part, men and women prefer different styles when it comes to decorating. Men are generally drawn toward:

- Decorating styles that are bold and uncluttered by accessories such as throw pillows and decorative objects.
- Color schemes that include black, brown, dark greens, red or navy.
- Fabric pattern choices like plaids and stripes.
- Upholstery choices like leather, nubby textures and sturdy weaves.
- Larger-scale furniture, which is more comfortable for them.
- Sturdy wooden furniture with clean lines and darker finishes.
- Furniture finishes and fabrics that are low maintenance and easy to keep clean.

Men's decorating tastes, however, can vary as widely as women's, so it's important that you choose a style that you find the most appealing and comfortable.

Make sure the room you're decorating reflects your own interests and personality. Are you a sports fan or a fishing fanatic? Are you outgoing or more reserved? Do you enjoy hanging out with a crowd or spending quiet evenings alone? Your home should be a reflection of who you are and the things you like

By following the practical tips and helpful suggestions in this decorating guide, you'll be able to create a space that is both comfortable and attractive—a place where you'll enjoy spending more time.

Start with a Plan

Before starting any new decorating project, take the time to decide how you need your space to function.

This task isn't complicated. It just takes some thought. If you plan to re-decorate the living room, take a few moments to decide what activities you'll be doing in the space. Will you be watching television? Do you need a comfortable conversation area for entertaining friends? How many people will you need to accommodate for seating?

Do you have enough space to include a game table or computer desk in the room, as well? Creating rooms with multiple functions is a great way to make more efficient use of your space.

Follow this same process for designing a dining room. Think about your entertainment needs for dinner guests or a "guys only" poker night. How many people are involved? How often do you hold each type of gathering?

What about the other rooms in your home? Do you want to use one of your bedrooms for a home office? Would the office also need to function as a guest bedroom?

Taking the time to consider the functional needs for your design project will help you decide what furniture pieces and lighting you'll need. Make a list of these items. Then, simply remove any pieces of furniture that don't meet your needs and replace them with ones that work.

Most of us have limited space in our homes, so it's important to use the space we have efficiently. Don't just "make do" with the current condition of your living areas. Take the time to figure out how you need your rooms to function and make them "work" for you.

Helpful Hints:

- If you want to add a new piece of furniture to your room, be sure to measure the space where you plan to place it to make certain it will fit. AND don't forget to measure the doors into your house and project room to make sure you can get the piece inside. If you plan to purchase a tall piece of furniture, measure the ceiling height in your room, as well.

- If your home office is small and needs to function as both an office and a guest bedroom, consider getting a daybed with a pull-out trundle bed underneath. It will provide sleeping space for two people and takes up less space than a sofa bed.

- If you have a formal dining room that's rarely ever used, consider making it a multi-functional room. With the appropriate storage units, it can also be a home office or hobby room. The dining table can be your desk or hobby table and a buffet or hutch can hide your computer, printer or hobby supplies.

Here's the Scoop

An organized, clutter-free home promotes a feeling of order and peace—a valuable commodity in today's chaotic world. Clutter has a way of sneaking up on us gradually until we feel overwhelmed and helpless in its wake.

It's important to get rid of the clutter in your home and keep only the items you need and enjoy. That's why every decorating make-over starts off by clearing everything out of the space, so you can start with a clean slate. You're less likely to bring the clutter back in to your newly decorated room.

Clearing out the clutter in your home and getting organized not only saves you time and money, it can help relieve some of the stress in your daily life and provide a more comfortable, relaxing environment.

So sort through all your stuff and get rid of everything but your "absolute must haves", then find creative ways to store or display them. This sounds like a daunting task, but it can actually be fun if you take a creative approach.

One way to make the most efficient use of your storage space is to buy containers or furniture units that will satisfy your storage needs and decorate your home at the same time.

The following is a list of some creative storage ideas for your home.

Living Room:

- Baskets are inexpensive but effective storage containers that can also add to your décor. They can hold magazines beside your favorite reading chair or a pile of logs on the fireplace hearth. Hang them on the wall to hold magazines, mail or keys.
- If you're planning to buy an ottoman, get a storage ottoman that can double as a coffee table and extra seating, as well.
- Bookcases can hold decorative boxes for storing small items in addition to books.
- If you need to buy bookcases, get the tallest ones your ceiling height will accommodate to get the maximum amount of storage for the least amount of floor space.
- Consider adding a narrow shelf around the entire perimeter of the room at door height to store books, decorative items and attractive storage containers.

Kitchen:

- Use a pot rack hung from the ceiling or wall to hold bulky items such as pots, colanders and ladles to free up space in cabinets and drawers.
- Store attractive dishes in a wall-mounted plate rack to decorate your kitchen and keep the dishes within easy reach.
- Hang mugs or cups from a peg rack on the counter backsplash or from cup hooks underneath the wall cabinets.

- Store dried staples (pasta, beans, sugar, etc.) in covered glass containers on the countertop to decorate the kitchen and free up space in the pantry.
- Use an attractive container on the counter to hold cooking utensils instead of storing them in a drawer.
- Store infrequently used items in baskets on top of the wall cabinets.
- Hang a small shelf for spices on the counter backsplash.
- Use recessed cabinets or shelves inside the space between the wall studs of interior walls. If you like, cover the opening with a framed print that is hinged on one side to act as a door.

Bedroom:

- Remove all clutter from underneath your bed. Save this space for under-bed storage containers.
- Get rid of the clutter on top of your dresser. Store jewelry in a jewelry box. Put loose change in an attractive dish.
- Clear out your closet. Donate or sell clothes, shoes or accessories that no longer fit, are out of style, or are in disrepair. Keep only the clothes you like and wear frequently.
- Use double racks in at least one section of the closet (one up high and one down low) to hang short items such as shirts and pants.
- Choose stackable containers for the closet to place either on the floor underneath hanging clothes or on the shelf above the clothing racks.
- Consider adding another shelf up high to store infrequently used items.

- Instead of a bench at the foot of the bed, choose a sturdy chest of drawers that can double as a bench as well as storage.
- Instead of bedside tables use small chests of drawers for more storage.

Miscellaneous Clutter:

- Home Office: Clear off the top of your desk. Store office supplies in your desk drawers, in a home office closet or in containers on a shelf. File paperwork in a filing cabinet. Clear off the clutter in your computer area. Store CD's in a CD holder. Hang shelves for manuals, directories and catalogs.

- Mementos: It's fine to hang on to a few very meaningful things, but if you have more than one or two boxes of these treasures, you may be going a bit overboard. Go through these items and weed out the things that are no longer important to you.

- Furniture: Is your home overcrowded with furniture you never use? Perhaps it was passed down from a relative, or maybe you recently made a move to a smaller place. If your furniture is not functional or you don't have the space for it, get rid of it. Imagine all the free space you'll have when it's gone.

Clear out the clutter in your home and invest in creative storage solutions that will help keep you organized and decorate your home at the same time.

Getting the Point

When planning your design project, make an effort to highlight an architectural feature in the room or create an attractive art arrangement on one of the walls that can serve as the room's focal point. You'll impress your guests with your decorating savvy and make the time you spend there more enjoyable.

The focal point can be a fireplace with attractive decorations hung above the mantel, a window with a nice view, artwork arranged over a sofa, or even an entertainment center, if the main function of the room is watching television instead of conversation.

If you have a nice view to the outside, make it the focal point of your room. Arrange the furniture to draw attention toward it. You might frame the window with drapery panels and place a tall plant on either side of the window to help make it stand out.

If the fireplace is a prominent feature in your living room, orient your furniture toward it. In the furniture layout in Figure 1 on page 10, the sofa is facing the fireplace, with two upholstered chairs across from it, creating a comfortable conversation area.

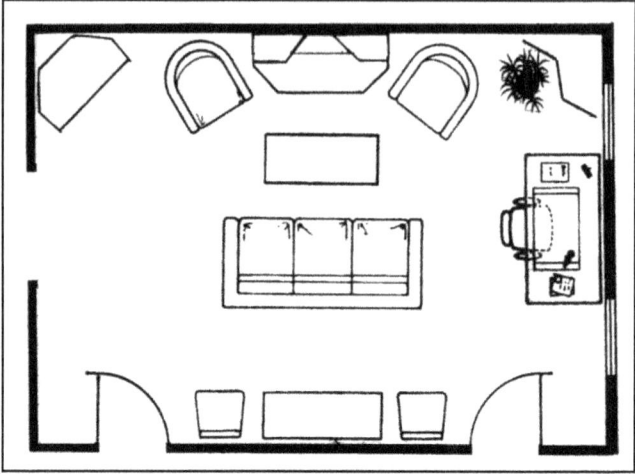

Figure 1

The focal point of any room should create sufficient impact to draw your attention. When using the fireplace as the focal point, arrange a group of accessories, such as framed mirrors or paintings, vases, candlesticks or other objects on or over the mantle shelf in order to create a pleasing composition to make your focal point stand out.

Try to make the grouping large enough in scale and extended high enough on the wall above the mantel to establish its importance. How do you know if your arrangement works? Just stand back and observe. Does the composition appear pleasing and relatively balanced? Does it create enough of an impact to draw your attention? As long as you're happy with the results and you've taken the time to check the overall impact, then go with it!

A good example for an arrangement above a fireplace mantle is a large painting hung above the mantel shelf, in the center, and two identical candlesticks or vases placed on either side of the painting. See Figure 2 on page 11.

Figure 2   Figure 3

You don't need to use a perfectly symmetrical arrangement of accessories over your fireplace mantle (called "formal balance") as shown in Figure 2. This type of composition creates a formal, traditional look. You can also create a more casual arrangement (informal balance) from a group of objects of varying sizes and shapes. With this type of arrangement, you'll need to do some experimenting with different combinations of objects until you feel the balance looks right.

An example of informal balance is a large framed mirror placed on the mantel shelf, slightly off center, which is balanced by a vase filled with tall branches. See Figure 3.

Painting an accent wall in a darker or more vibrant color is another way to make your focal point stand out. For example, if your focal point is a fireplace with white wood trim and mantle shelf, and your room is painted a neutral beige color, then painting the wall that the fireplace is on with a darker shade of beige (or one of your accent colors in the room, such as blue) will draw the eye to that wall.

Painting this accent wall will also make the fireplace "pop" because of the white paint of the wood trim against the darker wall color. Placing any object in front of a sharply contrasting color makes it more visible.

If you don't have a fireplace in your living room, you can create a focal point by arranging artwork over a sofa or an attractive piece of furniture, such as a chest or entry table. See Figure 4 below. Painting an accent wall in a contrasting color behind this arrangement will also create more impact for your focal point.

Figure 4

You can create a focal point for any room in your house, whether it's a prominent architectural feature, a window with an attractive view or an arrangement of artwork over a piece of furniture. Your home will score extra decorating points when you add appealing compositions for you and your guests to enjoy.

A Close Fit

Many homeowners tend to place all the furniture in the living room up against the walls, leaving a huge empty space in the middle of the room, which creates an awkward conversation area.

The seating arrangement for the living room needs to be close enough to carry on a comfortable conversation without having to yell at someone on the other side of the room. See Figure 5 below.

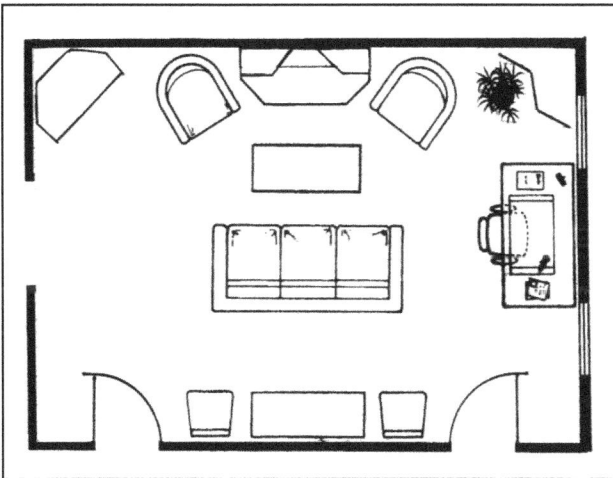

Figure 5

The furniture for a conversation group usually includes a sofa and two upholstered chairs, all facing each other, which makes it easier to see, as well as hear, the other members of the group. It is also convenient to have a coffee table in the center of the conversation area, as shown in Figure 5, placed close enough so your guests can easily reach a beverage from the table without getting up from their seats.

The furniture list you made when you decided on the function of your room will tell you how much seating you will need. You might prefer to have four upholstered chairs facing each other instead of a sofa and two chairs.

If you need seating for six to eight people on a regular basis, you might need two sofas and two chairs if your room is large enough to accommodate them. Whatever combination of seating you choose, try to group them in an arrangement that is comfortable for conversation.

By pulling your conversation-area furniture into a smaller, more functional group, you might be able to free-up space in the rest of the room for other activities (such as a game table or a computer desk) if space allows. Creating rooms with multi-functions is a great way to make more efficient use of your space.

Arrange the furniture you need in your living room to create a comfortable conversation area. When you're finished, stand back and take note of the distribution of the furniture throughout the room.

Do you have too many large (or visually heavy) pieces on one side of the room, making it feel out of balance? Do you have any empty corners that need to be addressed? If so, make a few adjustments and/or add objects as needed to try to make the room feel more balanced.

Look at Figure 5 on page 13. After pulling the conversation area furniture together into a smaller grouping, the homeowner placed a corner entertainment center and a desk in the room for additional activity areas, and then added a standing screen and plant to fill an empty corner.

Check your furniture layout for overall balance and add objects such as plants, screens, benches, small tables, etc. to any areas that might seem bare.

Furniture Arranging Tips:

A few furniture arranging tips are listed below that might be helpful when planning the furniture layout for your rooms.

1. Avoid lining all your furniture up against the walls, making your room feel like an office waiting area. Start by pulling your conversation area furniture into a tight group in the center of the room if the space is large enough, as shown in Figure 5 on page 13.

2. Try placing your furniture on the diagonal instead of square with the walls. Arranging the conversation area diagonally in your room can add a sense of motion instead of the static feel of furniture placed square with the walls. Repeating this angle with a few other furniture pieces in the room will create continuity. See the "before" layout in Figure 6 on page 16.

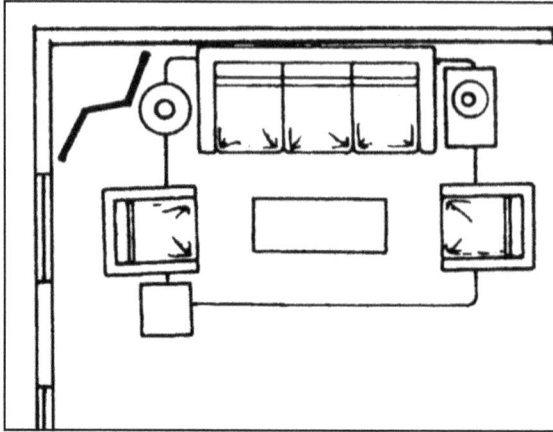

Figure 6

In Figure 6, the sofa and chairs are square with the walls. The sofa is flanked by an end table with a lamp on the right and a floor lamp on the left. A standing screen is placed in the corner. This furniture arrangement is functional, but it gives the room a rather static feel.

In the "after" layout shown in Figure 7 on page 17, the sofa is placed on an angle in the corner in front of the standing screen and a sofa table for displaying accessories. This arrangement creates the focal point of the room, since the space has no prominent architectural feature.

The sofa is flanked by an end table on the right and a floor lamp on the left. The chairs, as well as the area rug, are also placed on an angle. The coffee table was replaced by an ottoman which doubles as a coffee table, and also provides additional seating when needed.

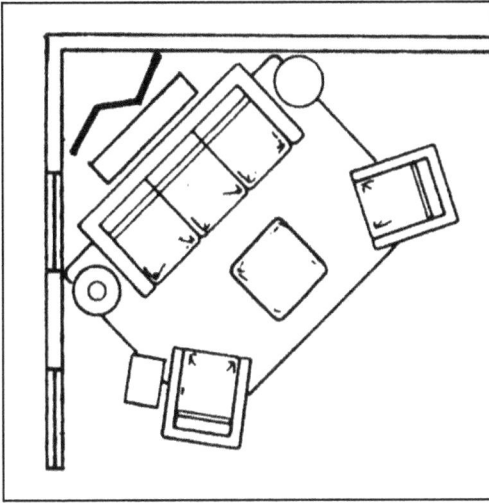

Figure 7

3. Try to balance the number of wood and upholstered pieces you use in the room. Too many hard surfaces make the space feel cold and uninviting. Use fabrics, plants, rugs, pillows, etc. to add softness and warmth.

4. If you don't have room to include end tables for lighting next to your sofa, pull the sofa away from the wall just far enough to place a long, narrow sofa table behind it to hold lamps and interesting accessories. See the example in Figure 7 above.

5. If the room is a long, rectangular shape, divide it into two or three separate activity areas, such as reading, watching television, or sitting by the fire. See Figure 8 on page 18.

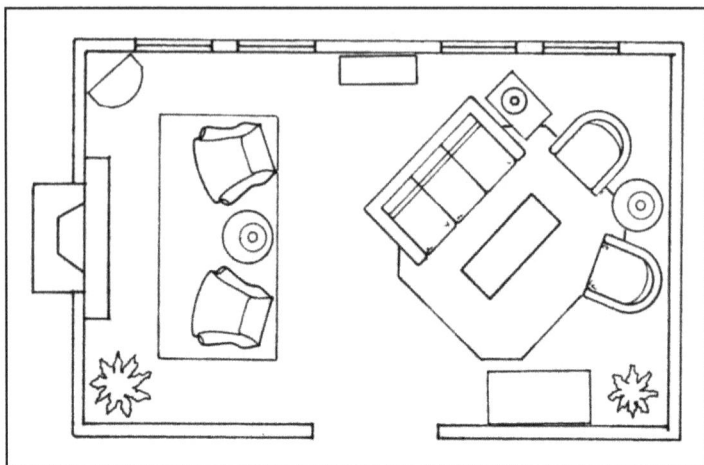

Figure 8

In the furniture layout above, the homeowner divided the long, rectangular room into two separate seating areas. On the left side of the room, two wing-back chairs were arranged in front of the fireplace for a relaxing place to read or enjoy the fire. A lamp was added to the table in between the two chairs for task lighting.

There is a comfortable conversation area on the right side of the room, placed on an angle to create a more welcoming approach from the room's entrance. An entertainment center was included in this area for watching television. Both seating groups were anchored with area rugs to help define the separate spaces.

Try rearranging the furniture in your living areas to create a more comfortable conversation area. Include the furniture that you need to make your space more functional. After creating your layout, check to see that the furniture is distributed evenly throughout the room.

Road Blocks

Does your current furniture layout make you feel like you're running through a maze of detours and road blocks? Blocking the flow of traffic is another common decorating problem that can cause a room to feel awkward.

Before creating a new furniture arrangement, take note of where the traffic patterns are in your room, so you'll remember to leave these areas free of furniture.

- Avoid placing any large pieces of furniture close to the entrance to the room which might create a road block for traffic.

- Make sure there is enough room for people to walk through the space comfortably without bumping into furniture. Traffic paths should be at least three feet wide if possible.

- Leave space for traffic to get from one side of the room to the other without cutting through the center of your conversation area. The ideal arrangement is to have the traffic flow around the perimeter of the room, if space allows.

Examples of living room furniture arrangements that might cause traffic flow problems are listed below:

1. Overcrowding your room with too much furniture. Solution: Refer to the furniture list you created when determining the function of your room. Remove any pieces of furniture that aren't absolutely necessary.

2. Using furniture that is too large for the space. Solution: Trade them out with smaller pieces in your home, purchase new ones that are more suitable in scale, or reduce the number of pieces in the room.

3. Pushing all the furniture up against the walls, forcing traffic through the conversation area, as shown in Figure 9 below.

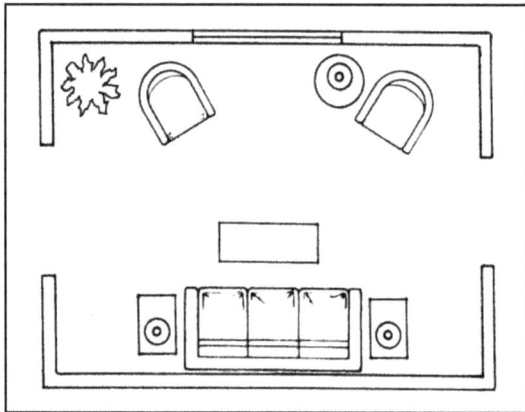

Figure 9

Solution: If your living room is too small to pull the furniture off the walls into a smaller conversation area that allows traffic to flow around it, then anchor the sofa against the longest wall, with the chairs perpendicular to the sofa, or opposite the sofa as shown in Figure 10 below. This will keep the conversation area together and allow traffic to flow around one side.

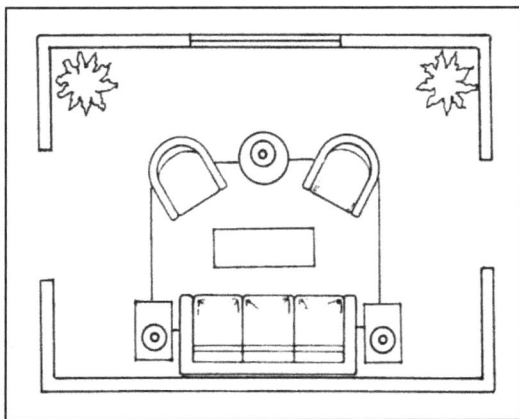

Figure 10

4. A sofa or chair that blocks the main entrance to a room. Solution: Rotate your seating arrangement, moving the offending sofa or chair to one of the walls in the room. It's usually best to place the sofa against the longest wall if the room is not large enough to float the seating area somewhere in the room. Try to avoid blocking the entrance to your room with a large piece of furniture.

Look at the before and after furniture layouts on page 22, showing an example of blocking the entrance to a room. In Figure 11, the sofa is blocking the room's only entrance. The furniture arrangement doesn't allow for easy access to the seating area.

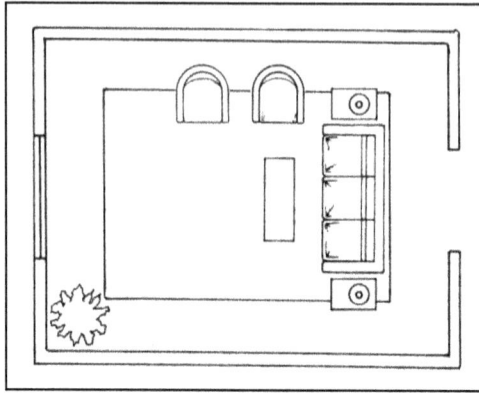
Figure 11

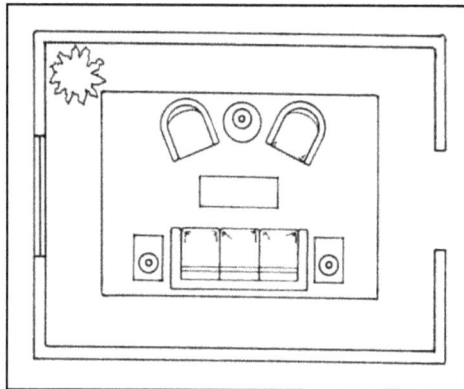
Figure 12

Figure 12 shows how the furniture layout was rotated to open up the entrance, creating a more welcoming feel. The club chairs were also repositioned across from the sofa, to provide a more comfortable conversation area.

Pay careful attention to where the traffic patterns are in your room, and place your furniture to promote a comfortable flow. Your furniture layout should draw you into the space—not put up a road-block in your path. Arrange your furniture so that it welcomes you into the room.

Slightly Off Kilter

Balance is a very important element when decorating a room. Whether referring to the placement of furniture, color or lighting, it's important to distribute them evenly throughout the space, or the room will feel off balance.

In addition to distributing the furniture evenly around the room, you should also check for balance in the height of the furniture pieces in the room. This doesn't mean that all the furniture pieces should be the same height. What you want is a mixture of heights—some tall objects and some low objects, to create an interesting mix.

After creating your furniture layout, simply check to see that the taller pieces are dispersed evenly around the room, otherwise, the room will feel out of balance.

If you have a tall piece of furniture on one wall, try to balance it on the opposite wall with another tall piece of furniture, or a lower piece of furniture with artwork arranged over it that will create enough visual weight on the wall to balance the taller piece of furniture.

We have already discussed distributing your furniture evenly around the room when arranging your furniture.

We also discussed creating a focal point by displaying decorative items on your focal point wall in an attractive composition that appears balanced.

Use this same technique to achieve balance for all the wall elevations in your room. A "wall elevation" is how the furniture appears when it is arranged in front of a wall. An example of creating balance on a wall elevation is listed below:

1. Start by placing the largest piece of furniture in the center of the wall. In this example, we'll use a sofa.

2. Add the next most important pieces, such as end tables on each end of the sofa. Try to keep them about the same height if they are not identical.

3. Arrange accessories, such as lamps, placed on the end tables. They can be identical pieces or visually balanced pieces (lamps that are not identical, but are equal in visual weight—see the explanation for visual weight on page 26).

4. Create a balanced display of artwork over the back of the sofa.

Look at Figure 13 on page 25. It shows an example of formal balance on a wall elevation where each side of the arrangement is identical.

You can also use furniture pieces, accessories and artwork that are not identical but are equal in visual weight to create informal balance on your wall elevation, as shown in Figure 14 on page 25.

Figure 13: Formal Balance on a Wall Elevation

Figure 14: Informal Balance on a Wall Elevation

Visual Weight:

When trying to create balance in your room, either in distributing the furniture evenly throughout the space or creating a balanced arrangement of furniture or accessories on a wall elevation, you need to consider the visual weight of the objects you plan to use in the grouping.

An example of comparing the visual weight of objects is two table lamps that are exactly the same height, but the base of one lamp is thin, like a turned wooden base, and the other has a fuller shape, like a Ginger jar. The lamp with the fuller-shaped base appears to have more visual weight than the thinner lamp base. Look at the example below.

You don't need to use identical lamps on the end tables beside a sofa, as shown in the formal balance example in Figure 13 on page 25, but check to see that the two lamps are fairly equal in visual weight and that they fit with the style of the décor and the colors or wood or metal finishes you plan to use in the room.

Comparing the Visual Weight of Furniture:

You will also need to consider visual weight when comparing furniture pieces, such as two living room chairs that have exactly the same dimensions, but one is a carved wooden arm chair with only the seat upholstered and the other chair is entirely upholstered. The wooden chair appears to have less visual weight than the upholstered chair.

In order to create balance between the two chairs, if you wanted to use them on either side of a fireplace, you would need to place another object, such as a small table, beside the visually lighter weight chair, as shown in Figure 15.

Figure 15

In addition to shape and mass, color and pattern also affect the visual weight of furniture:

- Bright, intense colors add visual weight
- Muted or neutral colors reduce visual weight
- Bold patterns add visual weight
- Solid colors or simple patterns reduce visual weight

Keep the visual weight factor in mind when arranging the furniture and accessories in your room. It isn't necessary to have perfectly symmetrical furniture arrangements on all your wall elevations, using identical objects on both sides of your composition, but try to keep the visual weight of your objects in balance.

Checking for balance, both in your furniture layout, as well as on your wall elevations will make your rooms more appealing.

The Power of Color

Color is a powerful decorating tool, and since the walls are the largest surface in any room, painting them is the least expensive but most dramatic change you can make. Color can completely transform the mood of any room, which affects the way you feel when you're in it.

You can use color to make a room feel bright or dark, cheerful or solemn, dramatic or casual, exciting or serene. Color can also create optical illusions to make small rooms seem more spacious or large rooms seem cozier. With the right color of paint, it's easy to camouflage a room's defects and highlight its positive features.

Even on a limited budget, appropriate use of color can bring a boring room to life. What mood do you want to create in your room? Choosing the right color scheme is simple once you make this decision.

Do you want to start your day in a bright yellow breakfast room? Do you prefer a soothing, serene green for your bathroom? What about a dramatic, rich burgundy for the dining room? Once you've decided on the color mood you want to use in the room, you're ready to select the specific colors for your color scheme.

Choosing Colors

You can create a color scheme from one color or several colors. When using more than one color, however, it's best to choose one of them as the predominant hue (the one you will paint on the walls), and use the other one or two colors as accents (for upholstery, window coverings and accessories). Try to distribute your accent colors evenly around the room for balance.

How do you pick the colors for your room? Just choose the ones you like or use the colors in the upholstered furniture you already own. You might also choose colors from an "inspiration piece", such as artwork, an area rug or a piece of fabric.

An easy way to choose your color scheme from an inspiration piece is to choose the lightest color in the artwork or fabric to paint the walls. Use one of the medium colors for a few of your solid-color upholstered furniture pieces and/or draperies. Pick one of the brightest colors for accents in the form of accessories, such as vases, throw pillows, frames, etc.

Colors fall into two categories: warm colors and cool colors. The warm colors are: reds, yellows and oranges. The cool colors are: blues, greens and violets.

If you want a very warm or a very cool color scheme, use an adjacent color scheme: two or three colors that are next to each other on the color wheel, like red, red-orange and orange or blue and blue-green.

For a more neutral color scheme, choose a complementary color scheme: two colors that are opposite each other on the color wheel, like red and green or blue and orange.

If you want a soothing mood for your bedroom or bath, don't paint the walls an energizing color like orange. The warm colors are more energizing. The cool colors are more calming, especially the pastel versions.

Neutral colors, such as beige and taupe are also more soothing. Paint the walls of your room a color that will create the mood you want.

If you want a particular theme for your room, such as Southwestern or tropical, then choose colors that are authentic to that style. A few palettes are listed below, but it's easy to gather this type of information from the Internet or books at your local library for any style you like.

Theme Room Colors and Styles

Seaside color schemes use aqua blue, sandy tan and sea glass green with touches of pale, driftwood gray. Furniture is casual and comfortable wicker, rattan or painted wood with sturdy fabrics or washable slipcovers. Window treatments are airy and light. Accessories include seashells of every size, shape and color, as well as nautical themed items, such as prints or figurines of wooden boats, lighthouses, fish, portholes, life preservers and beach scenes.

Southwestern colors are cactus green, adobe red and sand-colored neutrals with accents of bright yellow, dusty orange and turquoise. Hand-painted tiles are used on walls, floors and countertops. Accessories include wrought iron and pottery. Furniture is over-sized and made of rustic wood and iron, upholstered in sturdy woven fabrics, leather and suede.

Tropical color schemes include sky blue, olive green and warm brown with accents of red. Tropical décor features comfortable upholstered furniture and accessories made from animal and jungle prints, rattan, leather, wicker and grasscloth. Use bamboo or matchstick blinds or plantation shutters for window treatments. A few large palm or banana plants, jungle-theme lamps and large-scale accessories complete your theme.

Western style décor features honey colored wood, gray stone and black wrought iron metal. Accent colors can be brick red, terra cotta, forest green or navy. Western style furniture is often large scale and made of rustic wood. Fabrics and accessories include rock, wood, metal, leather, wool, birch bark, beadwork, weathered farm tools, old Indian blankets and antlers.

When choosing colors for your walls, remember that dark colors make things seem smaller and closer. Therefore, dark colors can make a room seem smaller. Light colors make things seem larger and farther away, so light wall colors can make a room appear bigger.

After you have chosen the paint color for your walls, it's best to test it before painting the entire room. First, paint a piece of poster board and hang it on the wall. Observe how the color of the paint is affected by the natural light coming into the room at various times of the day.

Also note how the artificial lighting in the room can change its appearance. If you're satisfied with your paint test, then go ahead and paint your room. If not, you'll need to make another choice.

If you aren't comfortable with a bold color change on your walls, add color to your rooms gradually. Use accent pillows, throws, area rugs and accessories to add color. Next, try painting one wall in a brighter color, as an accent or adding more color with window coverings.

Don't ignore the power of color when decorating your home. Painting the walls is an inexpensive way to make a dramatic change. And remember, it's just paint. If you don't like it, you can paint over it.

Try adding color to your living spaces, but choose your room's color scheme carefully, so it will have a positive effect on your mood and make the time you spend there more enjoyable.

Helpful Hints:

- When testing new paint colors or painting techniques, limit your commitment in time and money by trying them out in a small space first, such as a bathroom.

- When deciding whether to use a light or dark wall color in your room, keep in mind that objects are more visible when placed against a sharply contrasting color background.

  Dark furniture placed against a light-colored wall will stand out more. If you want to camouflage an object (such as a piece of furniture that is too large for the space), place it in front of a similar colored background.

- To make a group of framed prints or three-dimensional objects you want to display on your wall stand out, paint a block of color on the wall where they will be displayed. First measure the area where you will hang the wall art, then mark it off using painter's tape. It can be a rectangle or square just large enough to accommodate your grouping.

Paint inside the taped-off area using one of the accent colors for your room that will contrast with the wall art you want to display. Remove the tape before the paint is dry for cleaner edges.

If you're handy with a miter saw, you can also frame the edges of the painted area with molding. Hang your artwork and admire the results!

Keeping Things Under Cover

Window coverings dramatically affect the overall finished look of any room. There are hundreds of choices, including curtains, shades, blinds, shutters and valances. How do you decide which ones will work for your decorating project?

The most important thing to consider when choosing window treatments is the function they need to perform. Window coverings can provide privacy, block light, heat, cold or noise, as well as protect your furniture from the harsh rays of the sun. Make sure the window treatments you choose will perform the function you need.

Fabric window coverings help soften the hard, rectangular lines of windows. You can use them to create a focal point if your room doesn't have a prominent architectural feature. They can also hide problems with the size and shape of your windows, as shown on pages 55 - 57.

The window treatments you choose should fit the color and style of your décor. For example, if your decorating style is modern, don't choose country style café curtains for your room. And don't use formal, velvet draperies in a casual breakfast room.

Below is a list of some of the choices for window coverings:

Blinds: Some of the many types of blinds that are available include bamboo roll-up blinds (shown at right) or match-stick pull-up blinds which are more casual and create a tropical or Asian mood. Vertical blinds (shown below) are typically used for informal, contemporary décor. Venetian blinds (also shown below, combined with draperies) are more informal and are made from wood for a traditional setting or metal for a contemporary look.

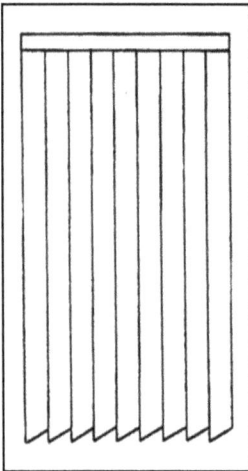

Vertical Blinds

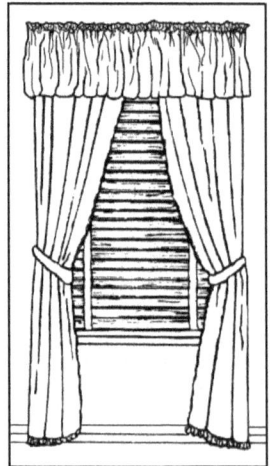

Venetian Blinds

Shades: Roman shades are flat panels of fabric that pleat when raised, as shown below. Balloon shades (also shown below) can be either pleated or gathered, and are used in traditional décor.

Roman Shade

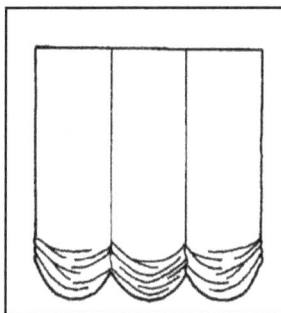

Pleated Balloon Shade

Shutters: Louvered wooden shutters, shown at right, are available in a variety of blade widths. The narrow blade shutters are more traditional and wide blade shutters work well for contemporary or tropical décor.

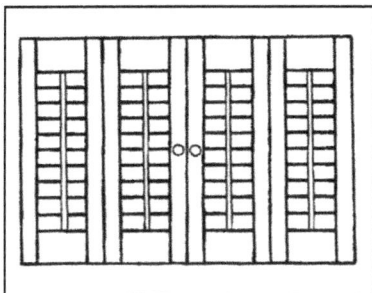

Draperies: Draperies (lined curtains) are made of heavier weight fabrics, like those shown on page 36. In this example, they are combined with Venetian blinds. They can be hung in a fixed position, or hung from hooks on traverse rods so they can be opened or closed. Draperies can be used in combination with just about any of the other window treatments, such as blinds, sheer curtains or valances.

Curtains: Curtains are unlined panels of fabric, either sheer or opaque, that can be pleated, gathered onto rods through rod pockets or hung from rings or tabs. They have a lighter, more casual look than draperies. Café curtains are hung from rings and cover only the bottom part of the window for a casual look.

Valances: Valances can be made of fabric or wood (cornice) and can be formal or informal depending on their fabric and shape, as well as how they are combined with other treatments. See the example on page 36, which shows a valance hung over drapery panels and Venetian blinds.

When choosing design motifs for curtain fabrics, upholstery fabrics, wall paper and floor coverings, it's best to use only one bold pattern in the room. Good choices for secondary prints would be smaller scale stripes, dots, checks and plaids that coordinate with your color scheme and style of décor.

Window coverings don't have to be expensive. There are a wide variety of ready-made curtain panels, valances and window shades available at discount stores and home improvement stores. You can also find them in mail-order catalogs and on the Internet.

The possibilities for window treatments are unlimited. Just remember to consider the function you need them to perform, as well as the style and color scheme of the room you're decorating when making your choices.

Shedding a
Little Light

Ineffective lighting is another common decorating problem that can affect the function of a room and make it feel uninviting. Proper lighting is not only functional, it can dramatically affect the room's overall appeal.

Plan the lighting for your room the same way you planned all the other parts of your design, by considering the function the lighting needs to provide and the mood you want it to create. Also check to see that your lighting is balanced throughout the space.

Function:

When planning for lighting, be sure to provide adequate light for the tasks you'll be performing in your room, such as reading, deskwork or hobbies that require good visibility. Table lamps, floor lamps and wall-mounted swing-arm lamps are good choices for task lighting.

There should also be enough general (or ambient) lighting in the room to prevent it from being too dark. Use fixtures such as chandeliers, torchieres (floor lamps that shine light upward), wall sconces, recessed down lights and track lights for general lighting. It's a good idea to have a dimmer switch on these fixtures so you can vary the level of light in the room.

Mood:

There are three ways you can use lighting to influence the mood of a room: by the general feeling of the illumination (how bright or dim the lighting is), by the style of the light fixtures and by the use of accent lights.

The general illumination has the greatest effect on the room's mood. A brightly lit room projects a more work oriented mood, such as the light needed in a kitchen. A dimly lit room is more intimate, such as the level of light desirable in a bedroom or formal dining room. Decide what mood you want to create in your space in order to choose the type of lighting that will work best for your needs.

The lighting fixtures that you select express a certain style or mood, the same as your furniture selections. Some fixtures, such as table lamps, chandeliers and sconces, are more traditional and some are more contemporary in style. Some are lavish and ornate; others are simple and casual. As with the furniture you selected, lighting fixtures should complement the mood and style of your décor. For example, a modern chandelier would not be suitable in style for a Victorian dining room.

You can provide accents of light in specific areas of a room to add a dramatic touch. This type of lighting is called accent lighting. A few examples are listed below:

- Use a floor can to shine light up through the foliage of a large plant

- Showcase a piece of art using a picture light or wall-washer (either ceiling mounted or portable floor light that shines light onto the walls)

- Use low-voltage rope lights (tiny lights inside a flexible plastic tube) on top of kitchen wall cabinets to provide indirect lighting

- Use a lamp on a table to brighten a dark corner

- Use rope lights inside shelving units or curio cabinets to highlight collectibles

- Use rope lights behind each curtain valance to provide a pleasant glow at night

Accent lighting not only highlights special artwork and brightens dark corners, it adds drama and interest to your overall design.

Lighting Fixture Choices:

The different lighting elements in a room need to work together to provide the right amount of light needed to perform specific tasks, as well as to achieve the overall mood you want in the room. Consider the following when planning for the lighting in your space:

- Add variety to your lighting plan. Use different types of lighting fixtures for different tasks. Some of the many options available include: table lamps, sconces, chandeliers, floor lamps, recessed down lights, wall washers (either ceiling mounted or portable floor can lights that shine light onto the walls), indirect lighting, low voltage rope lights and floor cans. Check out the many options available at your local home improvement store.

- Have the illumination in your room flow in different directions. Some fixtures project light upward (a torchiere or floor can light), some downward (ceiling mounted or recessed can lights in the ceiling) and some project light in all directions (a chandelier or table lamp with a translucent shade).

- Position lighting fixtures at different heights, from ceiling to floor—some at the ceiling, some on tables and some on the floor. Try to distribute them evenly around the room to create a more balanced feel.

- Plan for different levels of illumination in different parts of the room. Some areas should be bright (for reading), some less bright (for watching television). Use dimmer switches on general lighting, as well as task lighting to control the amount of light you want at different times.

Lighting is an important element to consider when decorating your space. Be sure to give it the time and attention it deserves.

Finishing Touches

The finishing touches to any decorating project are the accessories. This is the step where you can express your own unique style, using objects that you've collected over the years because they have special appeal. But it's important to use accessories that fit with the décor you've chosen for you room.

Pay careful attention to the accessories you add. Do they match the style of your room? Do those sleek, silver, contemporary picture frames stick out like a sore thumb on your rustic country mantle? With practice, you can train your eye to look for these details.

Hanging Wall Art:

Wall art accessories include paintings, framed prints, framed mirrors, wall screens and even some three dimensional objects such as sculptures, ornamental metalwork and sconces. Wall art is a very important part of the room's décor; therefore, it's important to display these pieces effectively.

A common tendency when displaying a piece of framed art is hanging it too high, so it looks like it's "floating" by itself on the wall. Hang wall art pieces low enough so they appear to be part of a grouping of furniture beneath them.

When displaying a piece of art over a sofa, hang it only about eight to ten inches above the sofa back. Figure 7 below shows an example of "floating" art. Compare it to Figure 8.

Figure 7

Figure 8

Wall art can help establish the focal point of a room. A focal point should create sufficient impact to draw your attention, such as a large framed mirror hung over a chest of drawers in the foyer or a painting hung over the fireplace mantel.

When hanging a large piece of wall art, check to see that its scale and shape are a good fit for the space where it will be hung. For example, the shape of the wall space above a sofa is usually a horizontal, rectangular shape. Therefore, the best shape for artwork to fit this space is a rectangular or oval shape, hung horizontally. If the wall space is square, use a square or round piece of artwork. The art in Figure 7 is not an appropriate shape for this space.

Next, check the size of the wall art. Does it appear to be too large for the scale of the sofa, or is it too small to create the impact you want? The art piece in Figure 7 is too small in scale for the size of this sofa.

If you don't have one piece of artwork that is large enough, use several smaller pieces in a grouping as shown below.

When arranging a group of framed prints or paintings, hang them close enough together so they appear to be one unit, but not so close that the space looks crowded. There is no magic formula for determining how far apart to place the artwork because it varies according to the size of the pieces. Just stand back and take a good look. Does the spacing feel right or does it need to be adjusted? Does the scale of the overall grouping fit the space you need to fill?

It's usually a good idea to choose a similar frame material for all the pictures in the grouping—gold, silver, wood, lacquer, etc. And take note of the frame styles, whether they are rustic, contemporary, traditional, etc. Do they fit with the style of the other furnishings in your room?

You can also mix framed prints or paintings with other interesting shapes such as framed mirrors, shelves, sculptures, etc. in one grouping. An easy way to create your layout is to trace the shapes of your frames or decorative objects onto paper, label them so you know which picture or object each one represents and cut them out. Use painter's tape to hang them on the wall and move them around until you get a look you like, then hang the wall art in place of each cutout.

Remember to balance the visual weight of the objects when creating your wall art arrangement. Avoid putting all the large objects on one side and the small ones on the other. It's also a good idea to place the larger objects on the bottom so the arrangement doesn't appear top-heavy.

Arranging Accessories in the Room:

The second category for accessories includes items such as vases, throw pillows, sculptures, plants and framed photographs, which are placed on the floor, tables, shelves or sofas and chairs. Remember to keep your decorating style in mind when choosing the type of accessories you want to include in your room.

To create continuity in your decorating scheme, repeat a color or pattern at least three times in the room. Whether it is a type of metal finish, a fabric print, or a geometric shape, try to repeat it several times throughout the space.

If the hardware on your cabinetry is bronze, repeat that finish in the lamp bases and picture frames. You can also use the same fabric from your window treatments on bar stool cushions or an ottoman.

Group similar objects together to create more of an impact for your display.

When displaying small items, group similar objects together to create more of an impact, as shown above. These might be objects made up of similar materials, such as silver, leather or wood; or theme-related items, such as baskets, carved wooden masks or sports memorabilia.

Scattering small items around the room creates a cluttered feel, so group these items together into collections. And remember, the smaller the items, the closer they need to be placed to the viewer.

If you display a collection of small framed photos on the top shelf of a tall bookcase, you won't be able to see them from such a distance.

Avoid overcrowding your displays. This also creates a cluttered feel, and the objects aren't being shown off to their best advantage. Simply choose a few items of various sizes, shapes, heights and textures that will create an interesting composition. To create your display, place the tallest object at the back and arrange the rest in descending order of size, so all the objects can be seen.

When displaying groups of framed photographs, it's best to use one type of material for all the frames in the group (wood, silver, copper, brass, lacquer, etc.) to create a cohesive look, but choose frames that fit with the decorating style of the room, such as modern or rustic country.

When decorating a bookcase with a mixture of books and accessories, try not to overcrowd the shelves or they will look cluttered. Instead, use the "one-third" rule: one third books, one third accessories and one third space.

During the accessorizing process, don't forget to address any empty corners in your room that might seem bare.

There are lots of creative possibilities for adding interest to these areas. A few suggestions are listed below:

- A tall plant or a smaller plant on a table

- A lamp on a table if the corner is dark

- A tall, decorative folding screen

- A lighted curio cabinet

Use accessories to create attractive arrangements throughout your home for you and your guests to enjoy.

Try to balance the soft and hard materials in your room. Too many hard surfaces make a room feel cold and uninviting. Use fabrics, plants, rugs, pillows, and upholstered furniture to add softness and warmth.

Area rugs are accessories for the floor. They add color, texture and design patterns to your space. They can also help define a conversation area and cover cold, bare floors.

Accessories add the finishing touch to any decorating project. Just remember to use objects that fit with the color and style of the other furnishings in your room.

Helpful Hint:

- If you want an object to stand out, such as a vase, place it against a sharply contrasting color background. If you want to camouflage an object that seems to over-power the room, such as a giant-screen television or large entertainment center, place it in front of a similar colored background.

Money-Saving Idea:

- If you want to hang a group of framed prints together in a wall display, but the frames are mismatched styles and colors, use a can of spray paint to unify their appearance. Spray paint comes in a wide variety of colors and finishes from metallic to stone. Simply remove the prints and glass, spray paint the frames, let dry and reassemble the pictures to create a cohesive grouping.

Decorating Tip:

- The fireplace mantel is like a small stage, elevated above the rest of the room. Therefore, it's the perfect place to showcase your collectibles and establish a theme for your room. Gather your favorite collection, whether it's African masks or Western gear and set the stage for your theme with an attractive mantle display.

Tricks of the Trade

There are many designer "tricks of the trade" that you can use to create optical illusions to make your room appear different than it actually is. Whether you want to change the size or shape of your room or windows, or want to double an image, or make an object disappear, follow the guidelines below to help camouflage the negative features and highlight the positive features in your room.

Changing Room Dimensions

If you aren't happy with the dimensions or architectural features of your room, there are several designer tricks you can use to change its appearance through optical illusions.

Does the room feel too small or too narrow? Does the ceiling feel too low? Knowing how to choose the right wall treatments, furniture, window coverings and flooring can make all the difference. Choose the options below that best fit your room's needs:

To make a small room feel larger:

- Use smaller-scale furniture.

- Use solid color upholstery fabrics or fabrics with small design motifs.

- Avoid crowding the room with too much furniture.

- Paint the walls a light color to make them appear to recede. Paint doors and trim the same color as the walls to unify the space.

- The window treatment color should blend with the wall color, not contrast with it. Use either a solid color or small print for the fabric.

- Use small scale window treatments.

- Don't break up the floor space with area rugs.

To make a large room feel smaller:

- Select larger-scale furniture and use plenty of pieces to keep the room from feeling empty.

- Light colored upholstery will make furniture appear bigger and fill the space better. Bright colors and bold design motifs also make furniture seem larger.

- Paint the walls a darker color and try to break up the space by painting wall moldings, baseboards and trim around doors and windows in a contrasting color.

- Use a different wall treatment on one or more of the walls, such as a painted accent wall, a wall mural or wallpaper.

- Use big and/or elaborate window treatments. Dark window treatments, like dark wall paint, will make the room appear smaller, but light window treatments will contrast with the darker walls to break up the space. Either choice is fine.

- Break up the floor space with area rugs. Large, bold design motifs for area rugs are fine as long as they don't compete with a different bold design pattern on the walls or furniture.

To make a narrow room feel wider:

- Paint the end walls a darker color to make them appear to "advance" and use light colors on the long walls to make them appear to "recede".

- Use a striped rug with the stripes running across the width.

- Cover one of the long walls with floor-to-ceiling mirrors in a small space such as an entry.

- In a long, narrow hallway, avoid hanging art on the side walls. Instead hang a painting or framed print at the far end.

To make a low ceiling appear higher:

- Accentuate the vertical lines in the room by removing any horizontal moldings or paint them the same color as the walls.
- If using wallpaper, apply vertical patterns from floor to ceiling.
- Window treatments should also continue from floor to ceiling to avoid cutting the vertical height.
- Paint the ceiling a light color (white is best) to make it appear to recede.
- Darker colors on the floors make them appear to be lower than they actually are.

To make a high ceiling seem lower:

- Accentuate the horizontal lines on the walls by painting the horizontal trim (crown molding, chair rail and baseboards) in a contrasting color.
- Use contrasting wallpaper prints and/or paint colors above and below the chair rail, dividing the walls into two horizontal planes. If you don't have a chair rail, use a wallpaper border to divide the two treatments.
- Paint the crown molding the same color as the ceiling, or use a wallpaper border, matching the background color of the border to the ceiling color.
- Paint the ceiling a darker color than the walls.
- Lighter colors on the floors make them appear to be higher than they actually are.

Changing Window Dimensions with Curtains

Make a short window appear taller by adding a valance above it, starting the bottom edge of the valance just below the top edge of the window, and the top of the valance extends onto the wall space above the window.

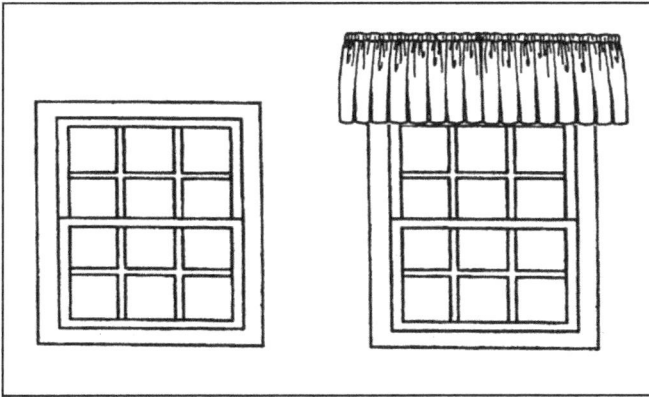

Make a tall window appear shorter by adding a valance, which starts near the top edge of the window and drops down to cover the top part of the window.

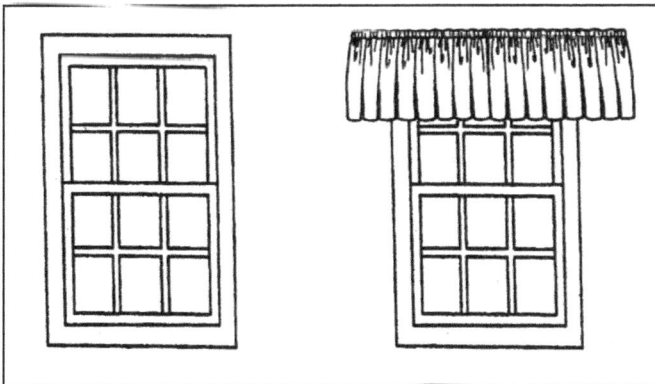

Make a wide window appear narrower by adding curtain panels to each side, starting close to the outside edge of the window and extending inside to cover some of its width.

Make a narrow window appear wider by adding curtain panels to each side of the window, which start at the side edges of the window and extend beyond the outer edges of the window onto the wall.

Adjust the heights of different size windows on the same wall by adding a valance that extends across the tops of both windows to make them appear the same height. Adjust their widths by adding curtain panels to each side to make them appear the same.

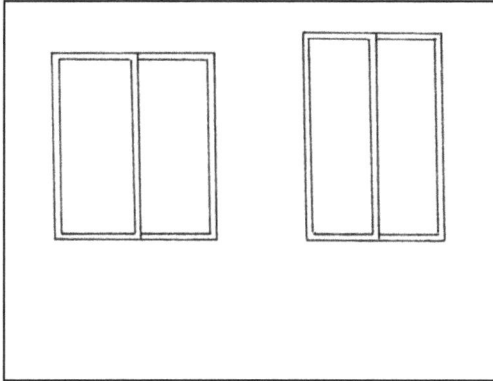

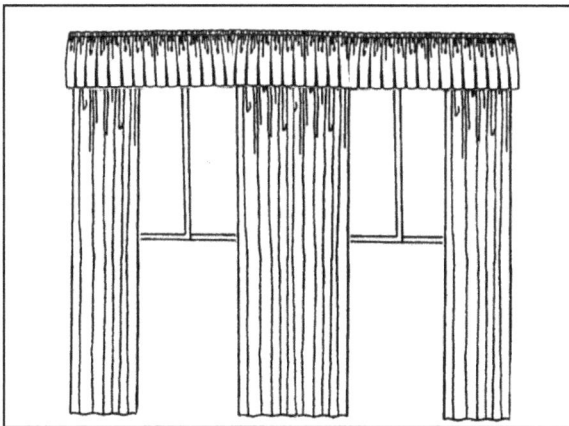

Designer Tricks
Using Mirrors

The unique characteristics of mirrors make them a very creative and useful decorating tool. Their reflective surfaces can increase the amount of light in your room, create optical illusions to make the space appear larger, or double the impact of any object they reflect.

Everyone knows that using wall-to-wall mirrors can make a room appear larger. Use any of the following techniques to achieve the results you want:

- In a narrow foyer, mirror an entire wall, which appears to double the size of the space.

- For very small spaces, such as a dining alcove, use mirrors on two walls that face each other. This produces the effect of infinite space because one wall reflects the other.

- If you want a soaring, two-story ceiling in your entryway, but yours is only eight feet high, cover the ceiling with mirrors to achieve the look of more height. (These mirrors should be installed by professionals for safety reasons.)

Decoratively framed mirrors can add a touch of style to any room, as well as being functional. A large framed mirror hung above a chest in a foyer, or over the fireplace mantel, can be the centerpiece of a focal point. Hang a group of small, framed mirrors together on a wall to create architectural interest.

Windowpane mirrors (a piece of wall art that looks like a window with a mirror behind it) can create the illusion of a real window on a blank wall. They come in a wide variety of shapes, sizes and decorating styles, and work great with any décor.

If your desk faces a wall without a window, hang a mirror on the wall in front of you that will reflect a more pleasing view behind you, such as a piece of artwork or a window with a view.

Another creative use for mirrors is to install them as a backsplash behind a stove. Not only are they easy to clean, but they reflect light into the work area and act as a rear-view mirror so you can see what's going on behind you. These can also be used as backsplashes over kitchen countertops, creating the same effect.

You can double the impact of your artwork or windows by placing mirrors opposite them to repeat the image from another angle in the room. Whenever you hang a mirror in a room, always check to make sure that it is reflecting a pleasant image.

In addition to being attractive accessories, mirrors are also functional. Hanging a mirror in the foyer makes it easy to check your appearance before leaving. Be sure to hang it at an appropriate height for viewing.

Mirrors can also be used to make objects "disappear". If you have an unsightly post standing in the middle of your room, which cannot be removed because it is structurally necessary, cover it with mirrors. They will reflect the objects in the room, making the post less noticeable. The same trick works for an over-scaled, square or rectangular coffee table or dining room table.

The Power of Illusions

When used effectively, these designer tricks can dramatically change the appearance of a room's scale or proportions to camouflage negative architectural features or accentuate positive features.

Which negative features in your room do you want to change? Which ones do you want to highlight? Now that you know how to use these tricks of the trade, you'll be able to make your rooms look their best.

What's Your Style?

Do you already have a clear idea about what style of décor you prefer? Do you want your furnishings to be casual and comfy or modern and sleek? Do you like a more formal, traditional setting or an eclectic mix of several styles? If you're not sure what decorating style you like best, then you need to do some research.

A good way to accomplish this is to visit furniture stores, wall paper stores, decorating fabric stores and paint stores. While there, take note of the prints, colors, finishes and styles that attract your attention. What is it about them that you like? Also pay attention to the ones you don't like and try to decide why they don't appeal to you.

You'll soon see a pattern developing for a particular style and palette of colors that you prefer.

Common Decorating Styles

The following is a brief description of some of the most common decorating styles used today. Which one appeals to you?

Country:

This style, ranging from log cabin to American farmhouse, has a more rustic theme that's all about casual comfort. It includes lots of texture, such as weathered woods and rough stone mixed with simple cotton fabrics in old-fashioned prints, plaids and denim. Window treatments are casual and simple. Accessories include antique collectibles, quilts, old toys, tools and dried wreaths.

Traditional:

This formal decorating style features heirloom-quality cabinetry, ornate moldings and fine fabrics, such as velvets, damasks and silks. Furniture is hand-carved from rich, dark wood, like cherry or mahogany.

The color scheme is drawn from deep, rich colors featuring navy, burgundy and forest green. Ornate accessories include shiny finishes, such as cut crystal, polished brass or silver as well as oil paintings in frames that are heavily carved and gilded.

Contemporary:

This style features furniture with clean lines, simple contours and strong horizontal elements. It calls for very few accessories, which are selected for their bold color and sculptural appeal.

Color schemes include neutrals, black and white, with accents of bright, bold colors. Shots of color are introduced in the form of an accent wall or in a geometric pattern on a rug or throw pillows.

Floor and table lamps have straight lines and metallic finishes or bold colors on sculptural bases.

Transitional:

This style incorporates furnishings from both traditional and contemporary décor. Transitional rooms are more casual than the formal traditional style with the less cluttered feel of the contemporary style.

Choose large, comfortable pieces of furniture that have the simple, straight lines found in contemporary décor. Add more traditional pieces that have soft, curved lines, like carved wooden tables and chairs. As in contemporary décor, limit the number of accessories, using just a few outstanding pieces.

Use objects that contrast in style, such as antique plates and contemporary paintings.

Eclectic:

Eclectic decorating mixes several different styles. The key is to use other elements, such as color and texture, to coordinate pieces from different periods.

It includes a harmonious mix of furniture, fixtures, and accessories that appeal to you. The most successful eclectic rooms incorporate only two or three different styles, but use a common decorating theme, such as color or shape to tie them all together.

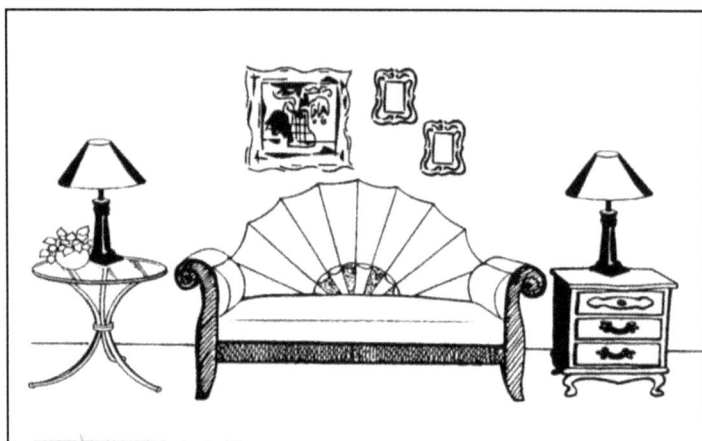

What decorating style do you prefer? With a little research you'll be able to discover the furniture styles, finishes, patterns and colors that appeal to you. Then your home will be a reflection of who you are and the things you like.

Quick Changes

If you're not ready for a major decorating redo, try a few of the following tips to give your rooms a quick change without spending a lot of money or time.

- Instead of painting the entire room, paint just an accent wall. Use a totally different color that contrasts, but also coordinates with your existing furniture. You might try a bright, cheerful color in the breakfast room, or maybe a darker, more dramatic color in the living room or dining room.

- Re-arrange the furniture in your room using the decorating guidelines presented in this book. You'll get a whole new look for zero dollars and very little time.

- If your upholstered furniture pieces are looking a bit worn or dated, cover them with slip covers. These are available in a wide range of prices at discount stores, home improvements stores, through mail order catalogs and online.

- Adding an area rug is another easy and inexpensive way to change the look of a room. Rugs are sold at a variety of discount and home improvement stores in a wide range of prices. They can add color and texture, help define a conversation area or completely change the room's style.

- Change the lampshades in your room. You can purchase inexpensive shades at many home improvement or discount stores. They can add life to old lamps and give your décor a whole new look.

- Accessories and wall art are the finishing touches in any room. Moving these pieces from one room to another can create a quick decorating change. Gather similar items that you have scattered throughout your home and display them together in one room to create a new theme. For example: arrange all your sports memorabilia in attractive displays in your home office or den.

- A new piece of wall art might be just the focal point your room needs. You can find inexpensive framed prints at many discount stores, craft stores, furniture resale stores or garage sales. Changing the accessories and wall décor is an easy way to give your room a quick makeover.

- Add accent lighting to create drama and brighten any dark corners. An inexpensive floor can placed behind a tall plant will create highlights and patterns on the walls and ceiling. Add a small picture light to emphasize a special piece of wall art. Place a string of low-voltage rope lights inside a curio cabinet to showcase collectibles. These are all quick, low-budget tricks that can add a bit of sparkle to any room.

Make your home an expression of your own personal style. Changing your décor doesn't have to cost a bundle. All it takes is a little time and effort.

Putting It All Together

We all want our homes to be functional, comfortable and attractive.

Taking the time to create a plan for how your rooms need to function and providing the necessary furniture and lighting to meet your needs will make your home more enjoyable and relaxing.

Adding the colors you prefer and the furniture and accessories that you find appealing will have a positive affect on your mood.

Use the suggestions, tips and guidelines presented in this book to create a more comfortable and attractive home that you will be proud to show off to family and friends.

Index

About the Author

Gloria Hander Lyons has channeled 30 years of training and hands-on experience in the areas of art, interior decorating, crafting and event planning into writing creative how-to books. Her books cover a wide range of topics including decorating your home, cooking, planning weddings and parties, crafting and self-publishing.

Gloria has designed original craft projects featured in magazines, such as *Better Homes and Gardens, McCall's, Country Handcrafts* and *Crafts*. She teaches interior decorating and event planning classes at her local community college. Visit her website for free decorating and crafting tips and recipes: www.BlueSagePress.com

Other Books by Gloria Hander Lyons

- *Easy Microwave Desserts in a Mug*
- *Easy Microwave Desserts in a Mug for Kids*
- *No Rules—Just Fun Decorating*
- *Just Fun Decorating for Tweens & Teens*
- *If Teapots Could Talk—Fun Ideas for Tea Parties*
- *Teapots & Teddy Bears—Fun Children's Tea Parties*
- *The Super-Bride's Guide for Dodging Wedding Pitfalls*
- *A Taste of Lavender: Delectable Treats with an Exotic Floral Flavor*
- *Lavender Sensations: Fragrant Herbs for Home & Bath*
- *Designs That Sell: How to Make Your Home Show Better & Sell Faster*
- *Self-Publishing On a Budget: A Do-It-All-Yourself Guide*
- *Hand Over the Chocolate & No One Gets Hurt! A Chocolate Lover's Cookbook*
- *The Secret Ingredient: Tasty Recipes with an Unusual Twist*

Ordering Information

To order additional copies of this book, send check or money order payable to:

Blue Sage Press
48 Borondo Pines
La Marque, TX 77568

Cost for this edition is $7.95 per book plus $3.50 shipping and handling for the first book and $1.50 for each additional book shipped to the same address (U.S. currency only).

Texas residents add 8.25% sales tax to total order amount.

To pay by credit card or get a complete list of books written by Gloria Hander Lyons, visit our website at:

www.BlueSagePress.com

www.ingramcontent.com/pod-product-compliance
Lightning Source LLC
Chambersburg PA
CBHW071843020426
42331CB00007B/1838